"RED SHADOWS"

THE HISTORY AND IMPACT OF COMMUNISM IN INDIA

AASHISH RAJ GIRI

Made with ♥ on the Notion Press Platform
www.notionpress.com

Contents

Preface

In this book, i have talked about how communism started in world and how it came to India, what are their contribution in India independence movement and what they gives to us till now... and why communism failed in India.......

- Aashish Raj Giri [argau43]
25/10/2023

ONE

HOW COMMUNISM STARTED IN WORLD AND PHILOSOPHY OF MARX, LENIN AND MAO

Communism means a principle or system of social organization based on all property being held in common, with actual ownership given to the entire community or state or a system of social organization in which all economic and social activities are controlled by one. A totalitarian state is dominated by a single and self-perpetuating political party.

The term "communism" was first used in English by Goodwin Barmby in a conversation with those he described as "Babeuf's disciples".

Karl Marx and other early communist theorists believed that hunter-gatherer societies, such as those found in the Palaeolithic period and horticultural societies such as those found in the Chalcolithic period, were essentially egalitarian and, therefore, they called their ideology primitive communism.

Primitive communism is a way of describing the gift economies of hunter-gatherers throughout history, where hunted or gathered resources and property are shared among all group members according to individual needs.

According to Harry W. Laidler, one of the first writers to believe in the primitive communism of the past was the Roman Stoic philosopher Seneca who said, "How happy were the primitive ages when the bounties of nature were the same...they kept all nature the same , which gave them secure possession of public property." For this reason he believed that such primitive societies were the richest because there was no poverty there. According to Eric van Ree, other Greco-Roman writers who expressed belief in a prehistoric humanity that had a communist-like social structure include Diodorus Siculus, Virgil, and Ovid.

Engels was the first to write in detail about primitive communism with the publication of "The Origin of the Family, Private Property, and the State" in 1884. Engels classified primitive communist societies into two stages: the "wild" (hunter-gatherer) stage which lacked a permanent superstructure and had close ties to the natural world, and the "barbarian" stage which had a superstructure like the ancient Germanic populations. . As far back as the Roman

Empire and the indigenous peoples of North America, prior to colonization by Europeans, inter-communal relations were egalitarian and matrilineal within the community.

The idea of a classless and stateless society based on communal ownership of property and wealth also permeated Western thought long before the Communist Manifesto. There are scholars who have traced communist ideas back to ancient times, particularly in the works of Pythagoras and Plato.

For example, followers of Pythagoras lived in the same building and shared their property because the philosopher taught complete equality of property and all worldly possessions were brought into a common store.

It is argued that Plato's Republic describes in great detail a communist-dominated society in which power is placed in the hands of an intelligent philosophical or military guardian class and the concepts of family and private property are rejected. . In a social system divided into the Homeric demos of warrior-kings and artisans and farmers, Plato envisioned an ideal Greek city-state without any form of capitalism and mercantilism, in which mercantile enterprise, political pluralism, and working-class unrest would be avoided. Should be considered as evils. Should be ended.

PHILOSOPHY OF MARX, LENIN AND MAO

KARL MARX - MARXISM

The term Marxism was popularised by Karl Kautsky, who considered himself an orthodox Marxist during the dispute between Marx's orthodox and revisionist followers. Kautsky's revisionist rival Eduard Bernstein also later adopted the term.

Karl Marx wrote: "At a certain stage of development, the material productive forces of society come into conflict with the existing relations of production or—this merely expresses the same thing in legal terms—with the property relations within the framework of which they have operated hitherto. From forms of development of the productive forces these relations turn into their fetters. Then begins an era of social revolution."

These inefficiencies manifest themselves as social contradictions in society which are, in turn, fought out at the level of class struggle. Under the capitalist mode of production, this struggle materialises between the minority who own the means of production (the bourgeoisie) and the vast majority of the population who produce goods and services (the proletariat). Starting with the conjectural premise that social change occurs due to the struggle between different classes within society who contradict one another, a Marxist would conclude that capitalism exploits and oppresses the proletariat; therefore, capitalism will inevitably lead to a proletarian revolution. In a socialist society, private property—as the means of production—would be replaced by cooperative ownership. A socialist economy would not base production on the creation of private profits but on the criteria of satisfying human needs—that is, production for use. Friedrich Engels explained that "the capitalist mode of appropriation, in which the product enslaves first the producer, and then the appropriator, is replaced by the mode of appropriation of the products that is based upon the nature of the modern means of production; upon the one hand, direct social appropriation, as means to the maintenance and extension of production—on the other, direct individual appropriation, as means of subsistence and of enjoyment."

The defining characteristics of Marxism have been described using the terms "Dialectical materialism" and

"Historical materialism", though these terms were coined after Marx's death.

The concept of dialectical materialism emerges from statements by Marx in the second edition postface to his magnum opus, Das Kapital. Which is an approach for explaining the transition from capitalism to socialism.

Historical materialism is the "view of the course of history which seeks the ultimate cause and the great moving power of all important historic events in the economic development of society, in the changes in the modes of production and exchange, in the consequent division of society into distinct classes, and in the struggles of these classes against one another."

----- *In the Marx view, human history is like a river. From any given vantage point, a river looks much the same day after day. But actually it is constantly flowing and changing, crumbling its banks, widening and deepening its channel. The water seen one day is never the same as that seen the next. Some of it is constantly being evaporated and drawn up, to return as rain. From year to year these changes may be scarcely perceptible. But one day, when the banks are thoroughly weakened and the rains long and heavy, the river floods, bursts its banks, and may take a new course. This represents the dialectical part of Marx's famous theory of historical materialism. — Hubert Kay, Life, 1948*

VLADIMIR LENIN - LENINISM

Leninism originally was neither a proper philosophy nor a discrete political theory. Leninism comprises politico-economic developments of orthodox Marxism and Lenin's interpretations of Marxism, which function as a pragmatic synthesis for practical application to the actual conditions (political, social, economic) of the post-emancipation agrarian society of Imperial Russia in the early 20th century.

As a political-science term, Lenin's theory of proletarian revolution entered common usage at the fifth congress of the Communist International (1924), when Grigory Zinoviev applied the term Leninism to denote "vanguard-party revolution."Leninism was accepted as part of Russian Communist Party vocabulary and doctrine around 1922, and in January 1923, despite objections from Lenin, it entered the public vocabulary.

In the early 20th century, the socio-economic backwardness of Imperial Russia (1721–1917) — characterized by combined and uneven economic development — facilitated rapid and intensive industrialisation, which produced a united, working-class proletariat in a predominantly agrarian society. Moreover, because industrialisation was financed chiefly with foreign capital, Imperial Russia did not possess a revolutionary bourgeoisie with political and economic influence upon the workers and the peasants, as had been the case in the French Revolution (1789–1799) in the 18th century. Although Russia's political economy was agrarian and semi-feudal, the task of democratic revolution fell to the urban, industrial working class as the only social class capable of effecting land reform and democratisation, in view that the Russian bourgeoisie would suppress any revolution.

In the April Theses (1917), the political strategy of the October Revolution (7–8 November 1917), Lenin proposed that the Russian revolution was not an isolated national event but a fundamentally international event—the first socialist revolution in the world. Lenin's practical application of Marxism and proletarian revolution to the social, political, and economic conditions of agrarian Russia motivated and impelled the "revolutionary nationalism of the poor" to depose the absolute monarchy of the three-hundred-year dynasty of the House of Romanov (1613–1917), as tsars of Russia.

MAO ZEADONG - MAOISM

The term "Maoism" is a creation of Mao's supporters; Mao himself always rejected it and preferred the use of the term "Mao Zedong Thought".

Maoism is a variety of Marxism–Leninism that Mao Zedong developed to realize a socialist revolution in the agricultural, pre-industrial society of the Republic of China and later the People's Republic of China. The philosophical difference between Maoism and traditional Marxism–Leninism is that a united front of progressive forces in class society would lead the revolutionary vanguard in pre-industrial societies rather than communist revolutionaries alone. This updating and adaptation of Marxism–Leninism to Chinese conditions in which revolutionary praxis is primary and ideological orthodoxy is secondary represents urban Marxism–Leninism adapted to pre-industrial China. Later theoreticians expanded on the idea that Mao had adapted Marxism–Leninism to Chinese conditions, arguing that he had in fact updated it fundamentally and that Maoism could be applied universally throughout the world.

In short It is a doctrine to capture State power through a combination of armed insurgency, mass mobilization and strategic alliances. The Maoists also use propaganda and disinformation against State institutions as other components of their insurgency doctrine.

TWO

HOW COMMUNISM STARTED IN INDIA AND THEIR ROLE IN INDIA INDEPENCENCE

HISTORY OF COMMUNISM IN INDIA

After the October Revolution in Russia, Bipin Chandra Pal and Bal Gangadhar Tilak were among the prominent Indians who expressed admiration for Lenin and the new rulers in Russia. Abdul Sattar Khairy and Abdul Zabbar Khairy went to Moscow as soon as they heard about the revolution. In Moscow they met Lenin and conveyed his good wishes to him. The Russian Revolution also influenced expatriate Indian revolutionaries such as the Ghadar Party in North America. The Khilafat Movement contributed to the emergence of early Indian communism. Many Indian Muslims left India to join the defense of the Caliphate. Many of them became communists while visiting Soviet territory. Some Hindus also joined the Muslim Muhajirs in traveling to Soviet areas. The colonial authorities were clearly troubled by the growing influence of Bolshevik sympathies in India. The first retaliatory move was to issue a fatwa, urging Muslims to reject communism. The Home Department established a special branch to monitor communist influence. Customs were ordered to check the import of Marxist literature into India. A large number of anti-communist propaganda publications were published.

The First World War coincided with the rapid growth of industry in India, resulting in the development of an industrial proletariat. Besides, the prices of essential commodities also increased. These were the factors that contributed to the formation of the Indian trade union movement. Unions were formed and strikes were organized in urban centers across India. In 1920, the All India Trade Union Congress was founded by S. A. Dange of Bombay. S. A. Dange published a pamphlet in 1921 titled Gandhi Vs. Lenin: On comparative study of the viewpoints of both the leaders, Lenin turned out to be the better of the two. In collaboration with local mill-owner Ranchoddas Bhavan Lotwala, a library of Marxist literature was established and translations of Marxist classics began to be published. In 1922, with Lotvala's help, Dange started the English weekly, Socialist, the first Indian Marxist magazine.

The Second Congress of the Communist International in 1924 emphasized that a united front should be formed between the proletariat, the peasantry, and the national bourgeoisie in the colonized countries. The 11th thesis was among the twenty-one conditions formulated by Lenin before the congress, which stated that all communist parties should support bourgeois-democratic liberation movements in the colonies. Some delegates opposed the idea of an alliance with the bourgeoisie and instead preferred to support the communist movements in these countries. His criticism was echoed by Indian revolutionary M.N. Roy, who attended as a representative of the Communist Party of Mexico. In the eighth condition, Congress removed the word 'bourgeois-democratic'.

The Communist Party existed in the 1920s and early 1930s, but was poorly organized, and in practice there were many communist groups operating with limited national coordination. The British colonial authorities had banned all communist activities, making the task of building a united party very difficult to. M.N Roy. A communist group was established in Tashkent on 17 October 1920, shortly after the Second Congress of the Communist International. M.N. Roy made contacts with Anushilan and Jugantar groups in Bengal. Bombay (led by S.A. Dange), Madras (led by Singaravelu Chettiar), United Provinces (led by Shaukat Usmani), Punjab, Sindh (led by Ghulam Hussain) and Bengal (led by Muzaffar Ahmed). Small communist groups were formed in.

Congress leader and famous poet Hasrat Mohani and Communist Party of India leader Swami Kumaranand were the first activists to demand complete independence (Purna Swaraj) from the British in the resolution of the All India Congress Forum at the Ahmedabad session of the AICC in 1921. Magfur Ahmed Ajazi supported the 'Complete Swaraj' proposal demanded by Hasrat Mohani.

The Labor Kisan Party of Hindustan was founded in Madras on 1 May 1923 by Singaravelu Chettiar. LKPH organized the first May Day celebrations in India, and it was the first time the red flag was used in India.

On 26 December 1925, the Communist Party of India was formed at the first party conference, first in Kanpur. S.V. Ghate was the first general secretary of CPI. The conference was held from 25 to 28 December 1925. Colonial officials estimated that 500 persons attended the conference. The conference was organized by a person named Satyabhakta, about whom very little is known. Satyabhakt is said to have argued in favor of 'National Communism' and against subordination under the Comintern. With the other delegates not voting, Satyabhakt left both conference venues in protest. The conference adopted the name 'Communist Party of India'. Groups like LKPH merged with CPI. The expatriate CPI, which perhaps had little organic character, was now replaced by an organization working inside India.

GROUPS AND ORGANISATION OF COMMUNIST AND THEIR ROLE IN INDIA INDEPENDENCE

1. Hindustan Socialist Republican Association

Following the Non-Cooperation Movement of 1919, the Hindustan Republican Association (HRA) was formed by Sachindra Nath Sanyal, Jadugopal Mukherjee and Jogesh Chandra Chatterjee after a meeting in Kanpur. HRA had branches in West Bengal, Agra, Allahabad, Banaras, Kanpur, Lucknow, Saharanpur and Shahjahanpur. Later, under the influence of Bhagat Singh, it became Hindustan Socialist Republican Association and decided that the new organization would work in cooperation with the Communist International.

They were also involved in making bombs in Calcutta – Dakshineswar and Shovabazar – and Deoghar in Jharkhand (then Bihar province). The most prominent attempt was the Kakori train robbery, where they looted government money from a train about 10 miles (16 km) from Lucknow. Key members of the HRSA were arrested and prosecuted for their involvement in that incident and other incidents that preceded it. The result was that four leaders – Ashfaqullah Khan, Ram Prasad Bismil, Roshan Singh and Rajendra Lahiri were hanged in December 1927 and the other 16 were imprisoned for long periods. The outcome of the trial, in which HRSA participants sang patriotic songs and displayed other forms of defiance, seriously damaged HRSA's leadership and dealt a major blow to its activities. Many people associated with HRSA who escaped trial were placed under surveillance or detained for various reasons. Chandra Shekhar Azad was the only prominent leader who managed to escape arrest while Banwari Lal became a government witness.

HRSA was against the Simon Commission. They bombarded the members of Simon Commission. After the death of Lala Lajpat Rai, who died due to lathicharge while holding a peaceful protest against the Commission, they bombed the Central Legislative Assembly in Delhi. He protested against the introduction of the Public Safety Bill and the Trade Disputes Bill, both of which were drafted in an attempt to counter revolutionary activities and the effects of trade unionism. After a trial, Singh, Sukhdev and Rajguru were hanged for their actions on 23 March 1931.

2. Communist Party of India

The Communist Party of India, a major communist party still in existence, was formed in Kanpur on 26

December 1925. S.V. Ghate was the first general secretary of CPI. Many communist groups were formed by Indians with the help of foreigners in different parts of the world, Tashkent contact groups were formed in Bengal along with Anushilan and Jugantar groups, and small communist groups were formed in Bombay (led by S.A. Dange in), Madras (led by Singaravelu Chettiar), United Provinces (led by Shaukat Usmani), Punjab, Sindh (led by Ghulam Hussain) and Bengal (led by Muzaffar Ahmed). The party was poorly organized in the 1920s and early 1930s, and in practice there were many communist groups operating with limited national coordination. The British colonial authorities had banned all communist activities, making the task of building a united party very difficult. Three conspiracy trials against the communist movement took place between 1921 and 1924; First Peshawar Conspiracy Case, Second Meerut Conspiracy Case and Third Kanpur Bolshevik Conspiracy Case. In the first three cases, Russian-trained Muhajir communists were prosecuted. However, the Cawnpore trial had greater political impact. On 17 March 1924, Shripad Amrit Dange, M.N. Roy, Muzaffar Ahmed, Nalini Gupta, Shaukat Usmani, Singaravelu Chettiar, Ghulam Hussain and R.C. Sharma was accused in the Kanpur Bolshevik Conspiracy Case. The specific charge was that as communists they wanted to "deprive the King of the sovereignty of British India by completely separating India from Britain by violent revolution." The pages of newspapers published sensational Communist schemes daily and for the first time people became aware of Communism and its principles and the objectives of the Communist International in India on such a large scale.

A communist conference was held in Kanpur on 25 December 1925. Colonial officials estimated that 500 persons attended the conference. The conference was organized by a person named Satya Bhakta. At the conference, Satyabhakt argued in favor of 'National Communism' and against subordination under the Comintern(short form of communist international). With other delegates not voting, Satyabhakt left the conference venue in protest. The conference adopted the name 'Communist Party of India'. Groups like the Labor Kisan Party of Hindustan (LKPH) merged with the CPI. The expatriate CPI, which probably had little organic character anyway, was now effectively replaced by an organization active inside India.

Soon after the Bengal Workers and Peasants Party conference in 1926, the underground CPI directed its members to join the provincial Workers and Peasants parties. All open communist activities were carried out through the workers' and peasants' parties.

In 1927, the Kuomintang attacked the Chinese Communists, which led to a review of the policy of building alliances with the national bourgeoisie in the colonial countries. The post-colonial principles of the Sixth Comintern Congress called on Indian communists to counter 'national-reformist leaders' and 'to expose the national reformism of the Indian National Congress and to oppose all the phrases of Swarajists, Gandhians, etc., about passive resistance' . However, the Congress distinguished between the character of the Chinese Kuomintang and the Indian Swarajist Party, and considered the latter neither a reliable ally nor a direct enemy. The Congress called on Indian communists to make use of the contradictions between the national bourgeoisie and the British imperialists. Congress also condemned WPP. The Tenth Plenum of the Executive Committee of the Communist

International, 3 July 1929 – 19 July 1929, directed Indian communists to break ties with the WPP. When the Communists abandoned it, the WPP broke up.

On 20 March 1929, arrests were made against WPP(Workers and Peasants Party), CPI and other labor leaders in several parts of India in what became known as the Meerut Conspiracy Case. Now the communist leadership was put behind bars. The trial proceedings were to last for four years.

By 1934, the main centers of CPI activity were Bombay, Calcutta and Punjab. The party had started expanding its activities to Madras also. A group of Andhra and Tamil students, including P. Sundarayya, were recruited into the CPI by Amir Haider Khan.

The party was reorganized in 1933 after the release of communist leaders from the Meerut trial. A Central Committee of the party was formed. In 1934 the party was accepted as the Indian section of the Communist International.

When Indian leftist elements formed the Congress Socialist Party in 1934, the CPI denounced it as social fascist.

The League Against Gandhism, initially known as the Gandhi Boycott Committee, was a political organization in Calcutta, founded by the Communist Party of India and others to launch militant anti-imperialist activities. The group took the name 'League Against Gandhism' in 1934.

In connection with the change in the Comintern's policy towards Popular Front politics, the Indian Communists changed their affiliation to the Indian National Congress. The Communists joined the Congress Socialist Party, which functioned as the left wing of the Congress. By joining the CSP, the CPI accepted the CSP's demand for a Constituent Assembly, which it had condemned two years earlier.

However, the CPI analyzed that the demand for a Constituent Assembly would not be an alternative to the Soviets.

In July 1937, a secret meeting was held in Calicut. Five persons were present in the meeting, P. Krishna Pillai, K. Damodaran, E.M.S. Namboodiripad, N.C. Shekhar and S.V. losses. The first four were members of CSP in Kerala. The CPI in Kerala was formed with the Pinarayi Conference on 31 December 1939. The latter, Ghate, a member of the CPI Central Committee, came from Madras. Contacts between the CSP and the CPI in Kerala began in 1935, when P. Sundarayya (CC member of the CPI, who was then in Madras) met EMS and Krishna Pillai. Sundarayya and Ghate visited Kerala several times and met CSP leaders there. Contacts were facilitated through national meetings of Congress, CSP and All India Kisan Sabha.

Cooperation between socialists and communists reached its peak in 1936–1937. At the Second Congress of the CSP, held in Meerut in January 1936, a thesis was adopted declaring that there was a need to create 'a united Indian Socialist Party based on Marxism–Leninism'. At the 3rd CSP Congress held in Faizpur, many communists were included in the CSP National Executive Committee.

In Kerala the communists gained control of the CSP and controlled the Congress there for some time.

Two communists, E.M.S. Namboodiripad and Z.A. Ahmed became the All India Joint Secretary of CSP. There were also two other CPI members in the CSP executive.

On the occasion of the Ramgarh Congress Conference of 1940, the CPI issued a declaration called the Proletariat Path, which sought to use the weak position of the British Empire during the war and called for general strike, no-tax, no-rent policies . To mobilize for armed revolutionary rebellion. The National Executive of CSP gathered in Ramgarh decided that all communists were expelled from CSP.

In July 1942, as a result of Britain and the Soviet Union becoming allies against Nazi Germany, the CPI was legalized. The Communists strengthened their control over the All India Trade Union Congress. Also, the Communists were politically sidelined due to their opposition to the Quit India Movement.

In 1946 The Communist Party of India was the only nation–wide political organisation that supported the rebellion which is known as Royal Indian Navy mutiny. The British authorities had later branded the Naval Mutiny as a "larger communist conspiracy raging from the Middle East to the Far East against the British crown".

The Communist Party of India opposed the partition of India and did not participate in the Independence Day celebrations of 15 August 1947 in protest against the partition of the country.

3. Naujawan Bharat Sabha

Naujawan Bharat Sabha (NBS) was founded by revolutionary Bhagat Singh in March 1926. It was a leftist Marxist organization that sought to promote revolution against the British Raj. The NBS was radical in its views related to religion, agrarian reform and agitation. The organization was noted for its members' involvement in the assassination of John P. Saunders(a British Officer) in December 1928. After that NBS organized a protest against Simon Commission in Lahore.

The association was banned in July 1929 during a period when the government imposed Section 144 to control meetings due to increased public support for the jailed Singh and his fellow hunger strikers. NBS members were involved in the campaign.

NBS worker Sohan Singh Josh was jailed for his role in the Meerut conspiracy case. The NBS became one of the three important leftist groups in Punjab, the others being the banned Communist Party of India and the Kirti Kisan Party. All three attempted an alliance and also tried to gather together various small leftist organizations. In September 1934, all organizations considered leftist were declared illegal under the Criminal Law Amendment Act (1908).

Notable leaders of NBS include Bhagat Singh, Karam Singh Mann, Sohan Singh Josh and others.

4. Kirti Kisan Party

The Workers and Peasants Party or Kirti Kisan Party was founded in 1925 in Bengal by Kazi Nazrul Islam, Hemant Kumar Sarkar, Qutbuddin Ahmed and Shamsuddin Husain as the Labor Swaraj Party of the Indian National Congress. WPP had great influence in Bombay, Punjab, Uttar Pradesh and Bengal. WPP representatives, together with Nehru, were able to persuade the AICC to make the Indian National Congress an associate member of the League against Imperialism. WPP was successful in organizing trade union action. It created unions among printing press, municipal and dock workers. It gained influence among the workers of the Great Indian Peninsular Railway. During 1928 the WPP led a general strike in Bombay, which lasted for months. Girni Kamgar Union was established at the time of the strike. During the protests against the Simon Commission, WPP played a major role in organizing demonstrations in Calcutta and Bombay. It also organized a 'Hartal' (general strike) in Bombay to protest against the Simon Commission. The party also worked for the abolition of the 'Zamindari' system in agriculture.

On 20 March 1929, arrests were made against WPP, CPI and other labor leaders in several parts of India in what became known as the Meerut Conspiracy Case. Most of the WPP leadership was now put behind bars. The litigation proceedings were to last for four years, thus ending the WPP. Bombay Chairman's WPP Tengadi died while the trial was still going on. Following the arrest of its main leaders, the WPP was dissolved.

Notable leaders of this party were Nares Chandra Sen-Gupta, Hemant Kumar Sarkar, Qutubuddin Ahmed, S.S. Mirajkar, Philip Spratt and many others.

Peshawar Conspiracy Case (1922–1927)

The Peshawar Conspiracy Cases were a group of five legal cases that took place in British India between 1922 and 1927. The Muhajirs, a group of Muslims, were inspired by the communist revolution and went to the USSR for training in the 1920s. Some of them returned to India from Tashkent in 1921 to instigate revolution. British intelligence got information about this from their foreign office and the police arrested the first group of revolutionaries and sent them for a sham trial.

The defendants in these cases had allegedly crossed into British India from the Soviet Union to promote proletarian revolution against British colonial rule. The colonial government feared that the defendants were entering India for the purpose of spreading socialist and communist ideas and supporting the emerging independence movement.

This was not the only case that became popular and inspired the imagination of the young population of the Indian subcontinent; There were some such cases. Among them, the Kanpur Bolshevik Case of May 1924 can be cited as a concrete case.

Kanpur Bolshevik conspiracy case

The Cawnpore Bolshevik Conspiracy Case was a controversial court case initiated in British India in 1924.

After Peshawar in 1922 another conspiracy cases were initiated by the British government, in Kanpur (1924). The accused in this cases included, important communist organizers working in India, such as S.V. Ghate, S.A. Dange, Muzaffar Ahmed and Akshay Thakur, and members of the expatriate party, such as Rafiq Ahmed and Shaukat Usmani.

On 17 March 1924, S.A. Dange, M.N. Roy, Muzaffar Ahmed, Nalini Gupta, Shaukat Usmani, Singaravelu Chettiar, Ghulam Hussain and others were accused as communists of "depriving the King of the sovereignty of British India by completely separating India from Britain by violent revolution." Wanted." "What was called the Kawnpore (now Kanpur) Bolshevik Conspiracy Case.

The case attracted public interest in the Comintern's plan to bring about violent revolution in India. "The pages of the newspapers published sensational Communist schemes daily and the people learned for the first time on such a large scale about Communism and its principles and the aims of the Communist International in India".

Singaravelu Chettiar was released due to illness. M.N. Roy was out of the country and hence could not be arrested. Ghulam Hussein confessed that he had received money from the Russians in Kabul and was pardoned. Muzaffar Ahmed, Shaukat Usmani and Dange were sentenced to four years imprisonment. This case was responsible for actively introducing communism to the Indian public.

After Cawnpore, Britain triumphantly declared that the affair had "exterminated the communists". But in December 1925, a conference of various communist groups was held in the industrial city of Cawnpore under the chairmanship of Singaravelu Chettiar. The main organizers of the meeting included Dange, Muzaffar Ahmed, Nalini Gupta, Shaukat Usmani. The meeting adopted a resolution for the formation of the Communist Party of India with its headquarters in Bombay (now Mumbai). Due to the extreme hostility of the British government towards the Bolsheviks, they had to decide not to function openly as a communist party, but chose a more open and non-union platform under the name of the Workers and Peasants' Parties.

Kakori Train Robbery

One of the successful attempts of the Hindustan Socialist Republican Association (then known as HRA) during the Indian independence movement against the British Raj was the Kakori train robbery on 9 August 1925 at Kakori, a village near Lucknow. The robbery was planned by Ram Prasad Bismil, Ashfaqullah Khan, Rajendra Lahiri, Chandrashekhar Azad, Sachindra Bakshi, Keshav Chakraborty, Manmathanath Gupta, Mukundi Lal, Murari Lal Gupta and Banwari Lal.

On 9 August 1925, down train number 8 on the Saharanpur railway line was going from Shahjahanpur to Lucknow. When it passed through Kakori, one of the revolutionaries, Rajendra Lahiri, used the emergency chain to stop the train. Later, other revolutionaries overpowered the guards. They looted only these bags (which were present in the guard's cabin and contained approximately 4600) which belonged to Indians and were being transferred to the British Government treasury. One passenger died unintentionally.

Following the incident, the British administration launched intensive searches and arrested several revolutionaries who were members or part of the HRA.

Their leader Ram Prasad Bismil was arrested in Shahjahanpur on 26 October 1925 and Ashfaqullah Khan was arrested in Delhi on 7 December 1926.

Lahore Conspiracy Case

On 20 December 1928, Bhagat Singh traveled in second class and Shiv Ram Rajguru traveled as his valet. They boarded the train and Bhagat Singh successfully left Lahore and reached Calcutta. Panditji (Chandrashekhar Azad) left with Kishori Lai from Lahore for Delhi on 25 December 1928 where Kishori Lai left him and returned to Lahore. A criminal case called the Lahore Conspiracy Case was registered, and the police swung into action by conducting raids and searches and making arrests. But Bhagat Singh, along with other revolutionary patriots, was planning an even greater task.

On 8 April 1929, at about 12.30p.m, when Sir George Chester stood up in the Central Assembly, New Delhi, to make an announcement regarding the exercise of special power by the Viceroy to pass the Public Safety Bill, Bhagat Singh and Batukeshwar Dutt who were The spectators, occupying seats in the gallery, stood up and threw two bombs one after the other near Sir Chester, not with the intention of killing him but with the intention of awakening the British government to reach out to the revolutionaries. There was complete chaos in the meeting. Bhagat Singh and Batukeshwar Dutt raised slogans of 'Inquilab Zindabad' (long live the revolution) and 'Down with the empire'. They also threw pamphlets in the meeting and surrendered voluntarily. A challan was presented against him in the court of ADM Delhi on 7 May 1929 under section 307 of the Indian Penal Code and section 3 of the Explosives Act. He was committed in the court of the Sessions Judge, Delhi. On 6 June 1929, Bhagat Singh read his detailed statement in the court. Asaf Ali was the defense lawyer. The verdict was announced on 12 June 1929 and both were sentenced to life imprisonment. Soon after, he was transferred to Punjab Jail to face trial in the Lahore Conspiracy Case. The judgment was upheld by the High Court on 13 January 1930, reported as Bhagat Singh and others vs. Emperor AIR 1930 Lahore 266.

A special tribunal was constituted and the right of appeal abolished. The trial before the tribunal began on 10 July 1930. Political prisoners raised patriotic slogans in the court. “Mera Rang De Basanti Chola, Maa, Mera Rang De Basanti Chola” was his favorite song which had a captivating effect on the youth. The verdict of Lahore Conspiracy Case was pronounced on 7 October 1930. Bhagat Singh, Rajguru and Sukhdev were sentenced to death. Kishori Lai Ratan, Sheo (Shiv) Verma, Dr. Gaya Prasad, Jai Dev Kapoor, Bijoy Kumar Sinha, Mahabir Singh and Kamal Nath Tiwari were sentenced to life imprisonment; Kundal Lai Gupta was sentenced to seven years’ imprisonment, while Prem Dutt was sentenced to five years' imprisonment. Three others were acquitted. Of the escapees, Chandra Shekhar Azad was martyred in an encounter with the police at Azad Park, Allahabad, in February 1931, while Bhagwati Charan died in a bomb explosion in May 1930, when she was rehearsing a planned bomb attack to escape. At 7 PM, Bhagat Singh, Raj Guru and Sukhdev were taken to the gallows. On March 23, 1931, they marched forward jubilantly shouting slogans like "Long live the Revolution", "Down with the Union Jack", "Down with British Imperialism".

Note:- Bhagat Singh was more revolutionary rather than communists and his guru and the party which he join was Anti-marxism.

Meerut Conspiracy Case (1929-1933)

The British government was clearly concerned about the growing influence of the Communist International and the infiltration of communist and socialist ideas among the workers by the Communist Party of India (CPI). The government's immediate response was another conspiracy case, Meerut. The conspiracy was to register a case.

In more ways than one, this trial helped the Communist Party of India strengthen its position among the workers. Dange, along with 32 other persons, was arrested on or about 20 March 1929 and tried under section 121A of the Indian Penal Code:

"Whoever, within or without British India, commits any offense punishable by section 121 or conspires to deprive the King of the sovereignty of British India or any part thereof, or by means of criminal force or show of criminal force conspires to intimidate the Government of India or any local Government, shall be punished with imprisonment for life, or imprisonment for a term less than ten years, or imprisonment of either description for a term which may extend to ten years."

Hunger strikes in Andaman

On 12 May 1933, some prisoners of the Cellular Jail gathered and started a hunger strike, leading to the death of Mahavir Singh, Mohan Kishore Namdas and Mohit Moitra. The British Raj accepted the demand of the freedom fighters to stop the hunger strike and ultimately the 46-day hunger strike ended on 26 June 1933. This marked the beginning of communist unification. This was the largest resistance group against British rule in the jail. They led a historic 36-day hunger strike in 1937, where the British government had to bow to the demands of political prisoners.

THREE

COMMUNISM IN INDIA AFTER INDEPENDENCE

On the eve of India's independence, the CPI was led by P.C. Joshi. Legal struggle was the party's main strategic strategy during Joshi's tenure as CPI general secretary, but the party also led radical mass struggles, notably the Telangana rebellion and the Tebhaga movement.

Party general secretary Joshi argued that independence was real and represented an achievement of the national bourgeoisie. But two other members of the CPI Politburo – B.T. Ranadive and Gangadhar Adhikari – argued that the transfer of power was a cosmetic move orchestrated by British imperialism.

Telangana Rebellion (1946-1951)

The Telangana movement represents the culmination of the efforts of the communist and socialist parties in the first few decades of the communist movement.

The tireless efforts to mobilize and organize farmers

against serious injustices represented a departure from traditionally more moderate reformist movements within the farmers.

Although the exact significance and value of the Telangana movement has been hotly debated, the role of the movement in bringing the farmers' question to the forefront of the communist movement cannot be denied; In actively organizing people against caste injustice; and fundamentally redefining the need for strong organizational structures, which was a key factor in the development of the movement.

By mid-1949 Andhra communists, based on their experience of the Telangana armed struggle, had begun to advocate that a 'Maoist' strategy for revolution was suitable for India. The following year the political line reversed once again.

The CPSU(Communist Party of Soviet Union) directed the CPI to abandon the Telangana struggle. In particular, the CPSU had begun to see Nehru as increasingly independent from America. Party gathered in Calcutta for a conference in 1947, which rejected the legacy of Ranadive (who had tried to imitate the Russian Revolution) and C. Rajeshwara Rao (who had tried to imitate the Chinese Revolution), and advocated peaceful methods of struggle. Changed the party line to elect. The conference adopted a new party programme, which recognized India as a 'dependent and semi-colonial country'. The 1951 program portrayed the Nehru government as "a government of landlords and princes and the reactionary big bourgeoisie collaborating with the British "imperialist".

The right wing of the party at the Madurai Party Congress opposed the 1951 party programme. The right wing wanted to recognize India as an independent country, and the use of terms such as 'semi-colonial' and 'dependent' should remove, the right wing of the CPI argued that Nehru favored independent development and an anti-imperialist foreign policy. The right wing of the CPI sought cooperation with progressive sectors within the Congress Party, including the government and the Indian National Congress. Proposed a joint struggle against Congress. The CPI Left, on the other hand, viewed the Nehru government as reactionary, and its supposedly progressive economic policies were illusory because the government defended feudal interests.

The Palghat Congress of the CPI in 1956 put forward a line of peaceful struggle and cooperation with the Nehru government.' The Palghat Party Congress reaffirmed the legal path of the party, and effectively abandoned the notion of armed struggle. Palghat Party Congress removed the description of India as a 'semi-colonial' country from the party program and instead stated that India had recently achieved its 'independence and sovereignty'. The CPI now supported the Government of India in its Second Five Year Plan, especially with regard to the development of heavy industries. The party now used more conciliatory language in relation to the Indian capitalists, as the fourth CPI party, the Congress Depicted the conflict between the forces of imperialism and feudalism on the one hand, and faced 'the entire Indian people, including the national bourgeoisie', on the other. . The new party line called for a national democratic front including national capitalists. The CPI's language regarding Indian foreign policy also changed significantly – Nehru was no longer branded as a puppet of American and British imperialism, but on the contrary praised the non-aligned policies of the Nehru government. The Fourth CPI Party Congress described the non-alignment policy as a 'sentinel for peace' and said that neutrality expresses the sentiment of the people to preserve their national independence.' Nevertheless, the Palghat Line argued that while the party should support the progressive policies of the Nehru government, the party should also struggle against the reactionary policies of the same government.

The CPI won the Kerala Legislative Assembly election of 1957, which was seen as a confirmation of the peaceful transition line set by the 20th CPSU Congress. The CPI's electoral victory in Kerala resulted in the first opposition-run state government in independent India. Namboodiripad was sworn in as Chief Minister. And while in the 1952 elections the CPI had won 106 seats in legislative assemblies across the country, in the 1957 elections the party won 201 seats across the country.

The victory in the Kerala elections led the party to ban militant mass movements across the country, leading to resentment among party workers in Kerala and other states.

While the formation of the Kerala state government in 1957 had strengthened the logic of parliamentary politics, the ousting of the Namboodiripad cabinet in 1959 reignited the debate on strategy and tactics within the party. After the Kerala Legislative Assembly elections of 1960, in which the CPI lost, Namboodiripad affirmed that the party would function as a constructive legislative opposition party.

Note:- With Communist Party of India there were three sections

1. Rightist (they were rightist amongst leftists)
2. Leftists (they were leftists amongst leftists)
3. Centre (they were centre amongst leftists)

Border Dispute: 1959

Longju incident

During the rebellion in Tibet in 1959, the CPI criticized the Nehru government for being biased in favor of the rebellion. A few months later, in August 1959, Nehru made a statement claiming that Chinese troops had entered Ladakh and the North-East Frontier Agency. As the border conflict emerged, there was a wave of condemnation within the CPI as critics tried to portray the party as China's fifth pillar. Many local units of the CPI called for a peaceful resolution of the border dispute. After the Longju incident, the CPI CEC(CENTRAL COMMITTE MEMBERS) resolution expressed confidence in China's non-aggressive character while expressing its commitment to India's territorial integrity and seeking a middle path. According to Nossiter, the proposal dissatisfied both the "Internationalist Left" and the "Nationalist Right" within the party. And on 7 September 1959, Zhou Enlai announced that China would follow the McMahon Line and but does not recognize.

Since the central CPI party leadership did not confront the public reaction by issuing a statement clearly supporting the territorial claims of the Government of India, discontent flared up in the party ranks (especially among the party's parliamentary representatives). Initially the dissidents managed to stay within the bounds of party discipline, but later their dissent escalated into open rebellion. Parliamentary representatives feared that if the party appeared to be taking China's side in the border dispute, If given, the party's progress in the 1957 elections would be reversed.

The CPI CEC met in Calcutta in late September 1959. A resolution was adopted which sought to find a balance between factions in the party, on the one hand affirming that the CPI would be in the forefront of India's defence, but also arguing that the crisis was being escalated by Indian reactionaries. The resolution did not reaffirm the McMahon Line as the boundary between the two countries. Soon after the Calcutta meeting, a five-member delegation led by Ghosh traveled to Peking to participate in the celebrations of the 10th anniversary of the People's Republic of China.

National Council meeting:- Meerut

In early November 1959, the CPI National Council met in Meerut. The Meerut meeting would last for a week. At the Meerut meeting the group hostile to China began to gain influence in the party. Dange reiterated his demand that the CPI should recognize the McMahon Line as the Indian border. The meeting adopted a 'nationalist' position on the McMahon Line as party policy became the basis of negotiations between the two countries, but The meeting also approved the 'internationalist' position that acceptance of territorial claims should not be a pre-condition for negotiations.

The CPI National Council met in January 1961. The meeting, inspired by Mikhail Suslov advice in Moscow to modify the CPI's anti-China policies, called for the withdrawal of the Meerut Resolution. Ghosh, supported by the rightists in the National Council, was able to defeat this demand.

CPI after Ghosh death

Ghosh died in January 1962, and his death brought to the fore questions over the party leadership. Dange and Namboodiripad both competed for the post of general secretary.

The CPI National Council met in April 1962 to decide how to resolve the vacancy of the General Secretary. There were sharp contradictions in the meeting. The Right insisted on Dange as the new General Secretary, the Left insisted on Refused to accept them. Ultimately the CPI National Council reached a compromise solution; Namboodiripad was named as the new general secretary while Dange was named as the party president (a new post created as part of the agreement). With 3 leftists, 3 rightists and 3 centrists. A new secretariat was formed. The inclusion of three additional secretariat members, P. Sundarayya, Surjit and Basu was a concession to leftist ideology.

Sino–Indian War

On 20 October 1962, a new border clash occurred, marking the beginning of the Sino-Indian War and again CPI members divided into two sides.

In the international sphere - on 25 October 1962 Pravda(USSR Communist newspaper) reversed its position (reportedly due to the Cuban Missile Crisis) and voiced support to China against India, calling for repudiation of McMahon Line and urging restraint among Indian progressives. But Party Chairman Dange and other right-wing leaders immediately condemned the Chinese actions and leftists were against it.

On 22 November 1962, the Indian government arrested approximately 1,000 leftists under the Defense of India Ordinance. Most of those detained were CPI leftists. Many remained in prison until late 1963. In Kerala, five former CPI ministers were among those arrested, among them the centrist Namboodiripad (who was released after a week).

The arrests further deepened the divisions in the CPI. The CPI leftists alleged that the right wing of the party had provided the list of leftists to the Home Ministry to facilitate the arrests.

February 1963 National Council meeting, The Right also took advantage of the absence of the Left to push for new resolutions at the CPI National Council meeting in February 1963. At this time, 48 of the 108 surviving National Council members were in jail or underground. In February 1963 a statement from the National Council again condemned Chinese 'aggression' and said that the CCP (Chinese Communist Party) had violated the principles of Marxism–Leninism.

Namboodiripad had tabled an alternative resolution at the meeting, titled Revisionism and Dogmatism in the CPI. Namboodiripad's document sought to highlight past and current errors, criticizing the rightist leadership for subservience to the Indian National Congress government and calling on CPI to remain neutral in the Sino-Soviet dispute. Namboodiripad's resolution was rejected by the National Council and Namboodiripad resigned from the post as general secretary of the party, citing his concerns with the 'nationalist' postures of the party. P. Sundarayya, Surjeet and Basu also resigned from the CPI Secretariat and CEC.

During 1963 the CPI was building a parallel party structure, with the Left, Gopalan, one of the key leaders. And the Left got a boost when many of their leaders were released from jail in late 1963. When many of the Left leaders of the CPI were released from jail in 1963, they faced a situation where The Dange group ousted him from his leadership duties. The Left reacted by grouping together and continuing to build their own parallel party structures.

After years of tension inside the party, the last straw were the so-called 'Danz Letters'. CPI leftist and independence journalist Dwijen Nandy found these letters when he was researching files in the National Archives of

India. Among four letters purportedly written by Dange in 1924, While he was in prison for political reasons and addressed the Viceroy of India, Dange sought to negotiate the terms of his release from prison.

If authentic, it would indicate that Dange had "offered to act as an agent of the British Government in return for remission of his prison sentence".

The letters caused outrage in the party and the CPI Left and some centrists demanded an investigation into the authenticity of the documents. S.S. Mirajkar, who was tried and sentenced in the Meerut conspiracy case along with Dange, claimed that he had seen the letters and confirmed their authenticity.

On 13 March 1964, the CPI Secretariat declared the documents a 'deliberate forgery' and accused the CPI Left of disseminating the documents. The Dange group claimed that the forged documents had been planted in the National Archives by a bourgeois agent.

The CPI CEC met on 9 April 1964. The leftists and centrists wanted to put forward an agenda point on the Dange papers. In contrast, the rightists wanted to put forward an agenda point on the disruptive activities of 'anti-party elements' (i.e. the CPI leftists). As soon as the meeting began, the Left and centrists demanded that the Dange letter issue be debated first and while the issue was being discussed, Dange should step down from presiding over the meeting. Dange refused to comply and 12 of the 27 CEC members left the meeting in protest. The CPI National Council met on 11 April 1964. Just two days earlier, the stage was set for the controversy about the Dange papers and role of Dange. During the debate on the papers, Dange again refused to vacate his chair, and 32 of the 65 National Council members present protested, accusing Dange and his followers of 'anti-unity and anti-communist policies'. And then left meeting. Subsequently, the National Council suspended the 32. Immediately after the suspension of the 32, the National Council sent leaders across the country to persuade state units to remain loyal. Dissidents were organizing party units across the country and announcing the expulsion of all Dange loyalists from the party. In June 1964 the CPI (Right) offered to lift the suspension of 32 National Council members if the Left dissolved its organizational structure. The last attempt to keep the party united was made at Gupta's residence on 4 July 1964. C. Rajeshwar Rao, Adhikari and Gupta, all CPI Secretariat members, sided with the right wing. Basu, Surjit and Promod Dasgupta participated from the left faction. The Left was willing to accept that Dange would be made the President if Namboodiripad was reinstated as General Secretary, but this proposal was rejected by the Right. Other issues were the right wing's demand that the left wing close their press outlets and the left's demand that scrutiny of party membership be initiated. But last attempt did not do anything thing and after that it was final tha CPI will divided into two groups. On 7 November 1964 a new party called CPI(M) Communist Party of India (Marxist) came out from CPI. The CPI supported the Indira Gandhi government during the Emergency and suffered a backlash when Gandhi was defeated in the 1977 election. Whereas CPI(M), by contrast, emerged victorious in 1977 state assembly elections in West Bengal and Tripura. Aftermath, Before the 1980 Lok Sabha elections, the CPI(M)-led West Bengal Left Front and the CPI entered into a seat-sharing agreement. In the same year, followers of Dange's pro-Indian National Congress line regrouped as the All India Communist Party. Dange himself was expelled from the CPI in 1981. Ahead of the 1982 assembly elections, the CPI joined the West Bengal Left Front.

The 1964 split remains a cause of contention between the CPI and the CPI(M), even though the parties are no longer political enemies.

Nexalite Insurgency

Naxalites are a group of far-left radical communists, who are supporters of Maoist political sentiment and ideology. Their origins can be traced to the split of the Communist Party of India (Marxist) in 1967, which resulted in the formation of the Communist Party of India (Marxist–Leninist).

The rebellion occurred during the height of the Sino-Soviet split, causing turmoil within communist organizations in India and the rest of the world. Revolt leader and ideologue Charu Majumdar theorized that the situation was ripe for launching an armed people's war in India after the Chinese Revolution (1949), the Vietnam War and the Cuban Revolution. Charu Majumdar wrote historic eight documents which became the foundation of the Naxalite movement in 1967.

The communists had already taken control of the Naxalbari area in 1965–66. The so-called "Siliguri Group" called for the beginning of an armed struggle, which led to the beginning of the rebellion. Many farmer cells were formed in the entire area. On 3 March 1967, just a day after the United Front ministers were sworn in in West Bengal, about 150 farmers, armed with bows and spears, took 300 maunds of paddy or about 11000 kg of paddy and started occupying the land. The farmers were angry that the CPI(M) did not keep the workers in the party. By March 18, farmers began confiscating land from jotedars (landlords who owned large plots of land in the area). Within four months farmers' committees were established throughout the region. The first clash between farmers and landlords occurred when a sharecropper, Bugul Kisan, was beaten up by the landlord gentlemen. Subsequently, peasant committees confiscated land, food grains and weapons from the landed elites, leading to violent clashes. The government began mobilizing police forces to deal with the rebellion.

On 18 May 1967, the Siliguri Kishan Sabha, whose president was Jangal Santhal, declared its support for the movement started by Kanu Sanyal, and declared its readiness to adopt armed struggle for the redistribution of land to the landless. At that time, the leaders of this rebellion were members of the CPI(M), which had joined the coalition government in West Bengal only a few months earlier. However, controversy arose within the party as Charu Majumdar believed that the CPI(M) had to support a principle based on revolution similar to that of the People's Republic of China. Leaders such as Land Minister Hare Krishna Konar were until recently "blatantly trumpeting revolutionary rhetoric, suggesting that militant confiscation of land was an integral part of the party's programme." However, now that they were in power, the CPI(M) did not accept it. Armed rebellion broke out, and all the leaders and many Calcutta supporters were expelled from the party. This disagreement within the party soon culminated with the Naxalbari rebellion on 25 May of the same year, and Majumdar led a group of dissidents to launch a rebellion.

On 25 May 1967, at Naxalbari in Darjeeling district, a sharecropper (tribal) of tribal background who had been granted land by the courts under tenancy laws was attacked by the landlord's men. In retaliation, the tribals started forcibly occupying their lands. When a police team arrived, a group of tribals led by Jangal Santhal ambushed them and a police inspector was killed by a volley of arrows. This incident encouraged many Santhal tribals and other poor people to join the movement and start attacking local landlords. After seventy-two days of rebellion, the CPI(M) coalition government suppressed the incident. Subsequently, in November 1967, this group organized the All India Coordination Committee of Communist Revolutionaries (AICCCR) under the leadership of Sushital Ray Choudhary. Violent revolts, like the Srikakulam peasant revolt, were organized in many parts of the country. By June, peasant committees seized land, ammunition and ammunition from the landholders in the areas around Naxalbari, Kharibari and Phansidewa. Food grains confiscated. Tea garden workers around the Darjeeling region participated in the strikes in support of the farmers' committees. The turmoil continued until 19 July when paramilitary forces were sent in by the government.

Mao Zedong provided the ideological inspiration for the Naxalbari movement, advocating that Indian farmers and lower-class tribals overthrow the upper-class government by force. A large number of urban elites were also attracted to this ideology, which spread through Charu Majumdar's writings, especially the landmark Eight Documents. These documents were essays drawn from the opinions of communist leaders and theorists such as Mao Zedong, Karl Marx, and Vladimir Lenin. Similar to the People's Court established by Mao, Naxalites prosecute opponents and execute them with axes or knives, beatings, or permanently deporting them.

On 22 April 1969 (Lenin's birthday), the AICCCR gave birth to the CPI(ML). The party was formed by CPI-M radicals like Majumdar and Saroj Dutta. Practically all Naxalite groups trace their origins to the CPI(ML).

In 1971, Satyanarayan Singh rebelled against the leadership, "personal killing of people branded as class enemies" and Majumdar's communalism. The result was that the party got divided into two parts, one CPI (ML) led by Satyanarayan Singh and one CPI (ML) led by Majumdar. The Naxalites gained a strong presence among the radical sections of the student movement in Calcutta around 1971. Students left school to join Naxalites. Majumdar declared that the revolutionary war would not only take place in rural areas as before, but would now take place everywhere and spontaneously. Majumdar thus announced a "line of destruction", stating that Naxalites should assassinate individual "class enemies" (such as landlords, businessmen, university teachers, police officers, politicians of the right and left) and others..

In 1972, the weakened and broken Majumdar died of multiple diseases while in police custody, possibly as a result of torture; His death hastened the fragmentation of the movement. His death was followed by a series of divisions throughout much of the 1970s. The Naxalite movement faced a period of extremely harsh repression that rivaled the Dirty Wars of South America, and the movement became even more fragmented. After the death of Majumdar, the CPI (ML) Central Committee was divided into pro- and anti-Majumdar factions. In December 1972, the central committee of the pro-Charu Majumdar CPI (ML) under the leadership of Sharma and Mahadev Mukherjee adopted a resolution to follow Charu Majumdar's line unconditionally, to which others did not agree. The pro-

Charu Majumdar CPI (ML) later split into pro- and anti-Lin Biao factions(Lin Biao was against USSR, he didnot want China to follow USSR order). The pro-Lin faction came to be known as the Communist Party of India (Marxist–Leninist) (Mahadev Mukherjee) and the anti-Lin faction later came to be known as the Communist Party of India (Marxist–Leninist) Liberation and was led by Johar, Vinod Mishra, Swadesh Bhattacharya. As a result of both external repression and failure to maintain internal unity, the movement turned into extreme communalism.

By 1978 the Naxalite peasant rebellion had spread to Karimnagar district and Adilabad district. This new wave of rebels kidnapped the landlords and forced them to confess to crimes, apologize to the villagers, and forcibly pay bribes. By the early 1980s the rebels had established a stronghold and sanctuary in the northern Telangana village and Dandakaranya forest areas along the Andhra Pradesh and Orissa border.

By 1980, it was estimated that about 30 Naxalite groups were active, with a total membership of 30,000. Although India's first wave of insurgent violence ended badly for this home-grown leftist extremist movement, it did not end the situations of everyone who inspired the movement or wanted to take up the Naxalite cause. This time, the rebellion was carried out in South India, specifically in the (undivided) state of Andhra Pradesh.

The Communist Party of India (Marxist–Leninist) People's War, commonly known as the People's War Group (PWG), was founded by Kondapalli Sitaramayya on April 22, 1980. He sought a more efficient structure in attacks and followed the principles of Charu Majumdar.

Incidets after 1980s.

On 12 February 1992, 37 or 38 people of the Bhumihar community were murdered in Bara village of Gaya district of Bihar. On 1 December 1997, believing that the village Dalits, mostly poor and landless, were Maoist sympathizers behind the Bara village massacre, the upper caste Ranvir Sena entered Laxmanpur Bathe village in Arwal district of Bihar and killed 58 Dalits. On March 18, 1999, 34 people of Bhumihar community were murdered in Senari village of Jehanabad district of Bihar.

The People's War Group (PWG) stepped up its attacks against politicians, police officers and land and business owners in response to the July ban on the group by the Andhra Pradesh government. Maoist Communist Center rebels intensified their armed campaign against Indian security forces after their leader was killed by police in December. An estimated 140 people were killed in fighting between the PWG and government forces throughout the year. According to government reports, 482 people were killed during the conflict in 2002.

Sporadic, low-intensity fighting between the PWG and government forces continued for most of the year. Attacks on police and Telugu Desam Party officials, believed to be carried out by the PWG, account for most of the major incidents and deaths. Talks between the government and the PWG failed due to a three-month ceasefire declared in late June. A few days after the ceasefire, an attack by the PWG threatened the ceasefire. More than 500 people were killed in sporadic, low-intensity fighting, a decline compared to previous years. Most of the victims were members of the police forces or the Telugu Desam Party (a regional political party).

The Communist Party of India (Maoist) was founded on 21 September 2004 through the merger of the Communist

Party of India (Marxist–Leninist) People's War (People's War Group) and the Maoist Communist Center of India (MCCI).

2005

In 2005, Violent clashes between Maoist rebels and state security forces and paramilitary groups escalated after peace talks between the PWG and the Andhra Pradesh state government broke down. The insurgents continued to employ wide-scale low-intensity guerrilla tactics against government institutions, officials, security forces, and paramilitary groups. For the first time in recent years, Maoist rebels launched two large-scale attacks on urban government targets. Fighting was reported in 12 states, covering most of South, Central and North India except the North-East and North-West of India. More than 700 people are reported to have died in violent clashes this year. More than a third of those killed were civilians.

In February 2005, the CPI (Maoist) killed 7 policemen, one civilian and injured several others during a massive attack on a school building in Venkatammanahalli village of Pavagada, Tumkur, Karnataka. On August 17, 2005, the Andhra Pradesh government outlawed the Communist Party of India (Maoist) and various mass organizations close to it, and a few days later began arresting suspected members and supporters. Among those arrested were former envoys to the 2004 peace talks.

On 13 November 2005, CPI (Maoist) fighters surprised the authorities by attacking Jehanabad in Bihar, freeing 250 captured comrades and capturing twenty captured paramilitaries and killing their leader. They also carried out several bomb blasts in the town. A jail guard was also reported killed.

2006

Maoist attacks continued, mainly on government and police targets. Civilians were also affected by landmine attacks affecting convoys of railway cars and trucks. Clashes between state police and rebels also resulted in the death of members of both sides and civilians caught in the crossfire. The fighting varies from state to state depending on the responses of security and police forces. Security forces in the state of Andhra Pradesh have been somewhat successful in maintaining control and countering Maoist insurgents. Chhattisgarh, the second state worst affected, has seen an increase in violence between Maoist rebels and villagers supported by the government. An estimated 500 to 750 people were killed in 2006, less than half Naxalites and about a third civilians.

More than 40,000 people were displaced in 2006. On 28 February 2006, Maoists attacked several anti-Maoist protesters in Erraboru village in Chhattisgarh using landmines, killing 25 people. On 24 March 2006, more than 500 heavily armed rebels attacked police camps in Udayagiri town in Gajapati district of Orissa, and freed 40 prisoners from the jail. On 16 July 2006, Maoists attacked a relief camp in Dantewada district, where several villagers were abducted. The death toll was 29.

On 18 October 2006, women from Maoist guerrilla forces blew up four government buildings in the Bastar region of Chhattisgarh. A day earlier, more than a dozen armed cadres of the group, supported by male associates, had blocked traffic on the Antagarh: Koylibera road in Kanker district, near Raipur city. They also detonated explosives inside four buildings including two schools in Kanker. On December 2, 2006, the BBC reported that Maoists had killed at least 14 Indian policemen in a landmine attack near the city of Bokaro, 80 miles from Ranchi, the capital of

Jharkhand state.

2007

In November 2007, reports emerged that anti-SEZ (Special Economic Zone) movements such as the Land Expropriation Resistance Committee in Nandigram, West Bengal, which arose following land expropriation and human displacement following the SEZ Act of 2005, have joined forces with the Naxalites. . To keep the police out since February. Police have found weapons of Maoists near Nandigram. Civilians were forced to choose between joining the Maoist insurgency or supporting Salwa Judum, and faced coercion from both sides. According to news reports, the conflict resulted in 650 deaths during 2007; Of these, 240 were civilians, 218 were security personnel and 192 were terrorists.

On 4 March 2007, Maoists shot dead a Member of Parliament (Sunil Mahato) of the Jharkhand Mukti Morcha (JMM) party from Jharkhand state. On 5 March 2007, Maoists shot dead a local Congress leader (Komati Prakash, local Mandal Praja Parishad (MPP) member) in Andhra Pradesh while he was inspecting a road construction project in Mahabubnagar district. However, police reportedly believe that Mahato's political rivals, including organized criminal groups, may be behind the murder. On 15 March 2007, an attack took place in the rebel stronghold of Dantewada in Chhattisgarh state. 54 people, including 15 Chhattisgarh Armed Forces personnel, were killed when 300 to 350 CPI (Maoist) cadres attacked a police base camp in Bastar region early Thursday. The remaining victims were tribal youth of Salwa Judum, who were designated as Special Police Officers (SPOs) and brought in to fight the Maoists. Eleven people were injured. The attack, which lasted for about two and a half hours, was led by the "State

Military Commission (Maoist)", which included about 100 armed Naxalites.

2008

On 16 February: A group of 50 insurgents armed with bombs and firearms, including women cadres, attacked a police training school, police station and armory in Orissa, killing 12 policemen and injuring 4. Before launching the attack, the Naxalites announced that they would not harm the public as their target was the police. On June 29: CPI(M) forces attacked a boat carrying 4 anti-Naxal police and 60 Greyhound commandos at Balimela Reservoir in Orissa. The boat sank, killing 38 soldiers, while 26 survived. After a two-week-long search, the bodies of a total of 38 Greyhound commandos and police personnel were found. They are still searching for 40 missing weapons. The attack comes just months after Andhra Pradesh Chief Minister YS Rajasekhara Reddy said that the elite commando force, which has the highest salary in the entire country, should get expand their operations to all affected areas and "things are more or less under control. From time to time, they (Maoists) indulge in high-profile attacks. On 16 July: A landmine hit a police van in Malkangiri district, killing 21 policemen. On April 13:- 10 paramilitary personnel were killed in an attack by Maoists on a bauxite mine in Koraput district in eastern Orissa.

2009

May 22: Naxalite guerrillas lured a police party into the forests of Gadchiroli district to investigate a road blockade and ambushed them, killing 16 policemen.

June 10: Nine policemen, including paramilitary personnel and a CRPF officer, were killed in a Naxalite attack during routine patrolling in an area considered a rebel stronghold inside the Saranda forest. Superintendent of Police Sudhir

Kumar Jha said: "Since the Naxals were aware of the geographical location and knew that the convoy would have to return from the same place, they had planted a powerful can bomb and ambushed the police vehicle."

June 12: 29 police personnel including Rajnandgaon District Superintendent of Police Shri Vinod Kumar Choubey were martyred which happened in Rajnandgaon.

June 13: Naxalites launched two attacks in broad daylight in and around a small town near Bokaro, killing 10 policemen and injuring several others using landmines and bombs. Two Naxalite guerrillas were also injured.

June 16: 4 policemen were killed and 2 others were seriously injured in an ambush by Maoists in Behrakhand in Palamu district. The guerrillas were reportedly waiting inside dense forests and as the policemen passed by them, they started firing indiscriminately, killing four of them on the spot.

June 16: At least 11 police officers were killed in a landmine attack following a shootout between police and suspected Maoist rebels. 7 rebels were also killed in the firing.

June 23: A group of armed Naxalite rebels riding a motorcycle opened fire at the Lakhisarai district court complex in Bihar and freed four of their comrades during a 48-hour bandh called by Naxalites to protest against increasing paramilitary activity in Langargh. One of the four rescued was Ghaskar Marandi, the zonal commander of Ranchi. On the same day, the Government of India banned the Communist Party of India (Maoist). Many, including the Left Front, opposed the ban, arguing that "all such organizations need to be brought back into the political mainstream."

July 12: At least 29 members of the Indian police were killed in an ambush by Maoist rebels in Chhattisgarh.

September 19: More than 50 Naxalites were killed and

around 200 were captured in a fierce gunbattle between Cobra and CRPF against Naxalites. 20 soldiers were reported missing.

September: Prime Minister of India Manmohan Singh acknowledged that the Maoists have growing appeal among a large section of Indian society, including tribal communities, the rural poor, as well as the intelligentsia and youth. He said that "dealing with left-wing extremism requires a nuanced strategy: a holistic approach. It cannot be treated merely as a law and order problem." 56 Maoist attacks were recorded in the first half of 2009. The South Asia Terrorism Portal reported 998 people killed in the conflict: 392 civilians, 312 security forces and 294 insurgents.

October 6: The body of a policeman abducted a week ago by Maoist rebels was found in Jharkhand.

October 8: At least 17 members of the Indian police, including a top commander, were killed in an ambush by Maoist rebels in Maharashtra. The fighting started after a group of Maoists attacked a police station in Gadchiroli district.

Major moist attack after 2010

On 6 April 2010 Naxalite rebels killed 76, consisting of 74 paramilitary personnel of the CRPF and two policemen. Fifty others were wounded in the series of attacks on security convoys in Dantewada district in the central Indian state of Chhattisgarh. The attack resulted in the biggest loss of life security forces have suffered since launching a large scale offensive against the rebels.

25 May 2013:- Naxal attack in Darbha valley resulted in the deaths of around 25 Indian National Congress leaders including the former state minister Mahendra Karma and the Chhattisgarh Congress chief Nand Kumar Patel.

25 May 2013:- Naxal attack in Darbha valley resulted in the deaths of around 25 Indian National Congress leaders including the former state minister Mahendra Karma and the Chhattisgarh Congress chief Nand Kumar Patel.
24 April: 2017 Sukma attack: Suspected Maoist rebels ambushed a group of Central Reserve Police Force officers who were guarding road workers in the Sukma district of Chhattisgarh. At least 25 CRPF soldiers were killed and 7 others were critically injured in the attack, which was one of the deadliest in recent years. Maoists killed 11 soldiers in a similar ambush in the same district at the beginning of March.

3 April: 2021 Sukma-Bijapur attack: : 22 soldiers including 14 Chhattisgarh policemen and 7 jawans of the CRPF, including 6 members of its elite CoBRA unit, were killed in a Maoist ambush on the border of Bijapur and Sukma districts in southern Chhattisgarh. One CRPF jawan was held captive by the Maoists.
29 July 2023: A fierce firefight erupts in the Suka district after Indian commando units entered a rebel controlled area. Indian security forces claim to have killed or injured 4-6 rebels, though no bodies are found.

Since 1997: 6,035–8,051 civilians killed and
1996–2018: 12,877–14,369 killed overall. [As per government]

Steps taken by government to eliminate moist insurgency

Goverment of India has launched three main schemes, "Special Central Assistance" (SCA) Scheme, "Security Related Expenditure" (SRE) Scheme, and "Special Infrastructure Scheme" (SIS) for the economic development of (LWE) Left Wing Extremism affected areas. As of July 2021, Rs 2,698 crore (US$375 million) has been released for 10,000 SCA projects, of which 85% were already completed.

The SRE specifically targets the "most affected" districts, under which Rs 1,992 crore (US$276 million) has been released since 2014. Various projects have been approved under the scheme, including 17,600 km of roads in two phases, of which Phase-I 9,343 km has already been completed, out of 5000 new mobile towers, 2343 are already operational and the remaining Will be operational by December 2022 (latest data is not available), Out of 234 sanctioned new Eklavya Model Residential Schools (EMRS), 119 are already operational, 1789 post offices out of total 3114 remaining will be ready by mid 2022(latest data not available), Financial inclusion of people affected by Left Wing Extremism 1077 ATMs and 1236 bank branches with 14,230 banking correspondents have been made operational. Under SIS, 400 fortified police stations have been established at a cost of Rs 1006 crore (US$140 million). Apart from this, funds have been released for schemes like helicopter hiring, media planning, police-public community activities and relations etc.

In July 2021, Madhya Pradesh has formed 23,113 women self-help groups covering 274,000 families in LWE (Left wings extremisms) districts, waived loans to tribals, provided land rights and land ownership documents to tribals, and opened 18 industries. Which will provide employment to 4000 people.

To counter moist insurgency several militias had been step up goverment and private individuals, like Salwa Judum(goverment sponsor militia in Chattisgarh), Sunlight Sena(private army by Rajputs and upper muslims in Bihar), Kuer Sena(private army of Rajputs in Bihar), Ranvir Sena(milita of Bhumihar and Rajput in Bihar), Bhumi Sena(private army of kurmi in Bihar) and Lorik Sena(private army of

yadav's in Bihar)
But after 2011 those milita which were working all were banned by Supreme court because because human rights activists failed case against Salwa Judum for violation of human rights and thereafter court directed state government to ban all these groups.

Irony:- Human rights activist don't says anything when cilvilan is killed by them(Moist).

In July 1971, Indira Gandhi took advantage of President's rule to mobilize the Indian Army against the Naxalites and launched a massive joint army and police counter-insurgency operation, dubbed "Operation Steeplechase", in which hundreds of Naxalites were killed and more than 20,000 suspects were arrested. And the cadres were imprisoned. In which senior leaders are also included. A brigade of paramilitary forces and para commandos also participated in Operation Steeplechase.

The governments of Andhra Pradesh and Orissa managed to crush the insurgents through a variety of counter-insurgency measures. Including with the help of Greyhounds, states established special laws that enabled police to capture and detain Naxalite cadres, fighters and alleged supporters. They also invited additional central paramilitary forces. States established rival mass organizations to attract youth away from Naxalites, initiated rehabilitation programs (such as surrender and rehabilitation packages, and established new informant networks. By 1994, about 9000 Naxalites surrenderer.

In 2003 an attack was made by moist on Chandrababu Naidu(at that time CM of United Andhra Pradesh and Telangana), aftermath the state began a rapid modernization of its police force by enhancing its technical and operational capabilities.

In 2022, the West Bengal state government and police acknowledged that there was a Maoist resurgence in the state, particularly in Jhargram, Purulia, Bankura, West Midnapore and Nadia. In May 2022, a new force named "Maoist Suppression Branch" was created by the Special Task Force of West Bengal Police.

SAMADHAN– The NDA government led by Prime Minister Narendra Modi, launched 'SAMADHAN' in May 2017. The acronym stands for the following: S – Smart Leadership, A – Aggressive Strategy, M – Motivation and Training, A – Actionable Intelligence, D -Dashboard Based KPIs (Key Performance Indicators), and KRAs (Key Result Areas), H- Harnessing Technology, A – Action plan for each theatre and N- No access to Financing.

Enabling laws: Laws like Rehabilitation and Resettlement Policy, 2007 and Forest Rights Act, 2006 are also aimed at providing the legal support to the people.

The government started the Backward Districts initiative in 2003-2004 and the Backward Regions Grant Fund (BRGF) under which 55 of the worst affected areas in 9 states were to be provided with funds to the tune of Rs. 2475 crores to tackle the problem of Naxalism.

FOUR

WHY COMMUNISM FAILED IN INDIA

Communism in India was always a failed experiment, a ruined belief dying a slow death. Working naturally contradictory to the original 'Idea of India', communism promotes authoritarianism and state control while encouraging undemocratic behavior. Communist states throughout the world put in place a set of rules that fundamentally contradicted Indian social hierarchies and undertones. History tells us that no ideology or belief has ever succeeded in thriving in India if it has failed to connect with the masses. Violence and terror never captured Indian society, unrest never blocked the steady flow of development. As happened with the communist flame, it gradually died out over time.

India is a fundamentally nonviolent society, which is structurally different from other centers of communist theory. The Hindu, Jain, and Buddhist ethics of nonviolence, ranging from "nonviolence toward all living things" to ahimsa, a form of nonviolent civil disobedience promoted and practiced by Mahatma Gandhi, made nonviolence apparently unfamiliar to most other cultures in Indian society. Has an importance. , In particular, Gandhi's advocacy and successful implementation of Satyagraha two decades earlier would have had a tremendous impact on its brainchild – the modern Indian state – in revealing the power of non-violent movements, leading people away from the Naxalite insurgency and retaliatory violence.

Western influences and adaptations, especially the democratic form of governance, played a significant role in alienating communism from the masses. Indian democracy deliberately acted in an anti-communist social manner, promoting political adversarialism and the multi-party system and promoting identity neutrality and non-selectivity. To this day India still detects substantial Western influences in society, ranging from the strong language power of the English language, industrialization, education system, establishment and parliamentary system, to the promotion of liberal nationalist ideals rather than violent socialist-communist belief. The constitutional framers chose a system that was fundamentally anti-communist in nature. Despite being socialist in economy, the country's well-functioning electoral democracy kept communists at bay and ensured cleanliness.

India's religious nature is quite unique compared to Asian countries that had experienced successful communist revolutions – India is secular but still deeply religious. Meanwhile, China and Vietnam have large irreligious or religiously unaffiliated populations, and Russia at the time of the Russian Revolution had a considerable secular or religiously unaffiliated population.

The inherently religious nature of daily life of almost all Indians probably contributed to the incompatibility of Indian society and communist appeals.

The failure of leadership in the Red Front – which proved to be a wheel in the machine of communism – severely stunted communist growth. The Indian communists lacked a dynamic, magnetically attractive, highly influential, democratizing and flexible non-autocratic leader capable of all kinds of resonance or even imitation, with a tendency to create conformity towards communism. Lenin, Mao, and Ho Chi Minh – even if not paragons of administrative leadership over a country – were great orators and revolutionary leaders who were renowned for their abilities to persuade and attract converts to the communist cause and to intelligently manage revolutionary efforts. Facilitated the rise of communism through And effectively. In contrast, Indian communism lacked any kind of genuine communist leadership. There were some leaders whose ideas and strategies were borrowed either from their masters or from their counterparts in Russia or China. There was no single leader with the original Indian model of communism as was the case with Mao for China, Castro for Cuba or Lenin for Russia. For example, Charu Majumdar, perhaps the most important communist leader, particularly idolized Mao's vision and strategy, but he failed to replicate the successful nature of Mao's revolution.

Their anti-national approach are also main reason why their ideology didn't succeed in India, like I will explain this to you with latest examples with regard to India....

1. Supporting Palestinians is humanity but supporting our kashmiri pandits is Communal!
2. Hamas is fighting for their religion but RSS is a terrorist

group!
3. Standing for Al-Aqsa mosque is religious stand but you stand for ram temple then it's again communal!
4. Treat everyone equal(as per basics idea of Communism) but they need reservation also!

Even before Independence, during the Second World War, in 1939, when the USSR and Nazi Germany were on the same side, undivided Communist Party of India (CPI) refused to oppose Hitler. However, when Hitler invaded Soviet Union in June 1941, Moscow told Indian communists that the real fight was between fascism and the Allies. Therefore, they should support the British in their war effort. After that, The Bengal famine of 1943 was a famine that occurred in the Bengal province of British India (now Bangladesh and West Bengal India) during World War II. It is estimated that 2.1–3 million people out of a population of 60.3 million died from starvation, malaria and other diseases aggravated by malnutrition, population displacement, unsanitary conditions and lack of health care. The famine was anthropogenic (man-made), wartime colonial policies were created and then exacerbated the crisis. The British government was responsible for this crisis and the death of 30 lakh people but the communist group in Bengal did not offer a single help and did not criticize the British for the terrible famine of Bengal. Communists came forward to praise the war efforts of the British government.

As above I already mentioned in "History of communism in India after independence" that leftists Communist blamed Indian government for creating trouble elements in ladakh beside not condemning china move. And in sino-indo war CPI(leftists) openly supported China.

CPI(M) stood against the Pokhran tests conducted by India. CPI(M) supported North Korea becoming a nuclear power, but for this it stood against its own country India. Initially, when Pokhran happened where India became a nuclear power, the CPI(M) excuse was non-proliferation and all kinds of humanitarian concerns, but the hypocrisy and double standards of the CPI(M) were exposed almost a decade later when North Korea conducted a nuclear test. . , According to the CPI(M) mouthpiece, North Korea had the legitimate right and legitimate need to conduct nuclear tests. The CPI(M) placed the blame for North Korea's actions on the United States. Kerala Chief Minister Pinarayi Vijayan also praised Kim Jong-un for his tough anti-America stance.

Inside the campus of JNU(Jawaharlal Nehru University) Delhi, several left parties students wings are active like All India Student Association (AISA), All India Student Federation (AISF) , Democratic Student Union (DSU) and Democratic Student Federation (DSF). Sometimes to hurt the religious sentiments of the society, they prepare nude and objectionable posters of Gods and Goddesses on their computers and paste them on the wall. Students belonging to these organizations mourned the hanging of Parliament attack convict Afzal Guru, they celebrated the killing of CRPF jawans in Dantewada, Chhattisgarh, they asked for beef in the hostel mess, they replaced Goddess Durga during the 'Navratri' festival. Worshiped 'Mahishasur' and they also invited Kashmiri separatist leader Syed Ali Shah Geelani for the meeting, however, JNU authority banned it. Professors who lean towards communist ideology inside the campus are also no different from these student groups. The professor runs the agenda of disintegrating India, the most ancient civilization, through his teaching.

A lady professor XYZ(Nivekita Mekok) while teaching large

group of students that Kashmir to not belong to India , aazadi slogans are rightly being raised by Kashmiri muslims and India should be giving freedom to Kashmir.

In the year 2016 a event was organised on 9th February to celebrate anniversary of terrorist Afzal Guru who was involved in the terrorist attack on Parliament. ABC (Canhaiya Cumar) was a member of AISF and was the President of JNU Students Union. Only ABC (Canhaiya Cumar) was involved in this incident. Anti-national slogans like "Bharat tere tukde honge inshallah inshallah" were also raised during the programme. Desi colleagues of JNU accused the Supreme Court judges of giving death sentence to terrorist Afzal Guru. Slogans were raised against the Supreme Court judges "Afzal, we are ashamed, your murderer is alive".(Afzal Guru, Sharminda hai kuki tere katil Zinda hai).

They are the same communist who used to say that army in Kashmir raped kashmiri women.

In 2017, during the Doklam standoff the frictions between India and China were high and India was in no mood to back off. Instead of supporting India ,the Communist Party of India- Marxist stood up with China. CPI-M stressed that India must allow Bhutan to take the lead in the negotiations with China and take a step back. Perhaps the idea of the CPI-M was that China to sway over Bhutan and take away the land which was in contestation. Not only did the political party took China's side but also pinned the blame on the Indian government for the dispute. The reason they gave was "India has openly sided with the US position on the South China sea, India has opposed the Belt and Road initiative. Within the country the Modi government has increased the profile of Dalai Lama and the so called provisional government, which are serious irritants for

China".

On June 16, 2020, 20 brave Indian Army soldiers were martyred for the motherland during a violent clash with Chinese troops to defend the area. They fought bravely and the Chinese side suffered 43 casualties. But instead of boosting the morale of the Indian Army and criticizing China and the Chinese military for the move to occupy the other's territory, the Communist Party of India-Marxist organized a protest against the Narendra Modi-led BJP government on June 16. When it comes to the rift between Indian and Chinese soldiers, the communist parties always lean towards the Chinese side by betraying their own nation.

On June 20- 2020, an All India Party meeting was being held under the chairmanship of Indian Prime Minister Narendra Modi on the India-China border issue in Ladakh. It was expected in the meeting that all political parties irrespective of their ideologies would move towards the Center and leave aside their differences and come together as it was a question of national integrity. But sadly, there were three political parties who decided to go against the national interest and adopt an anti-government stance at this crucial time. It was no surprise that two of the three political parties were Communist Party of India and Communist Party of India Marxist. In the All India Party meeting, instead of blaming China, the Communist Party of India accused the Modi government of getting closer to America. CPI's D Raja said that "we need to resist attempts to drag us into their alliance". The Communist Party of India did not speak a single word against China. There is a rift going on between the United States and China and America is looking for allies to stand against China, India can fulfill the need of the United States. Relations between

America and India have never been so close in history. It is not surprising that the Marxist Communist Party has come together with the CPI. CPI-M's Sitaram Yechury stressed the principles of Panchsheel to deal with China. Blaming the Indian government for the tensions between India and China itself reflects the priorities of the communist parties that currently rule India.

These are only some point which shows how they are anti-nationalist, because of all these things Communism never succeed in India.....

Conclusion:- In current scenario Communism didn't succeed because of their utopian vision, their arm struggle is also not for a good society. If in reality they want to succeed in India then they have to drop their anti-national approach and they have to stand with country first and belive in democratic government.

ALL THE SOURCE OF INFORMATION ARE FROM WIKIPEDIA AND SOME OF ARTICLE.

THIS IS MY FIRST BOOK AND I AM HAPPY AFTER WRITING THIS BOOK.

AASHISH RAJ GIRI, EAST CHAMPARAN- BIHAR

www.ingramcontent.com/pod-product-compliance
Lightning Source LLC
LaVergne TN
LVHW090135160826
845673LV00017B/2481

* 9 7 9 8 8 9 1 8 6 1 1 6 9 *